This book belongs to:

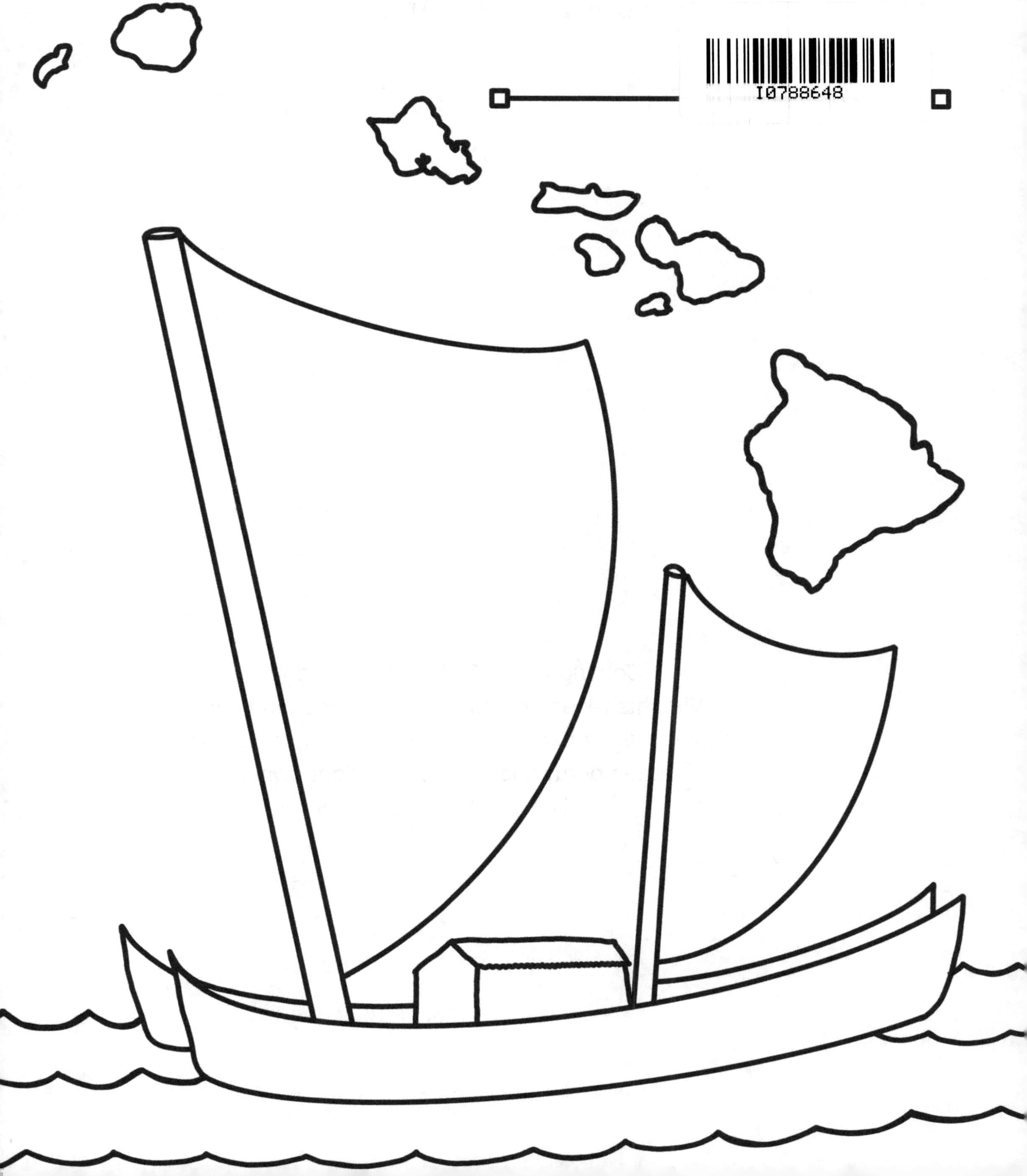

Color and Learn in ʻŌlelo Hawaiʻi Series
Book 1: Ocean Animals
Book 2: Island Animals

DOLPHIN

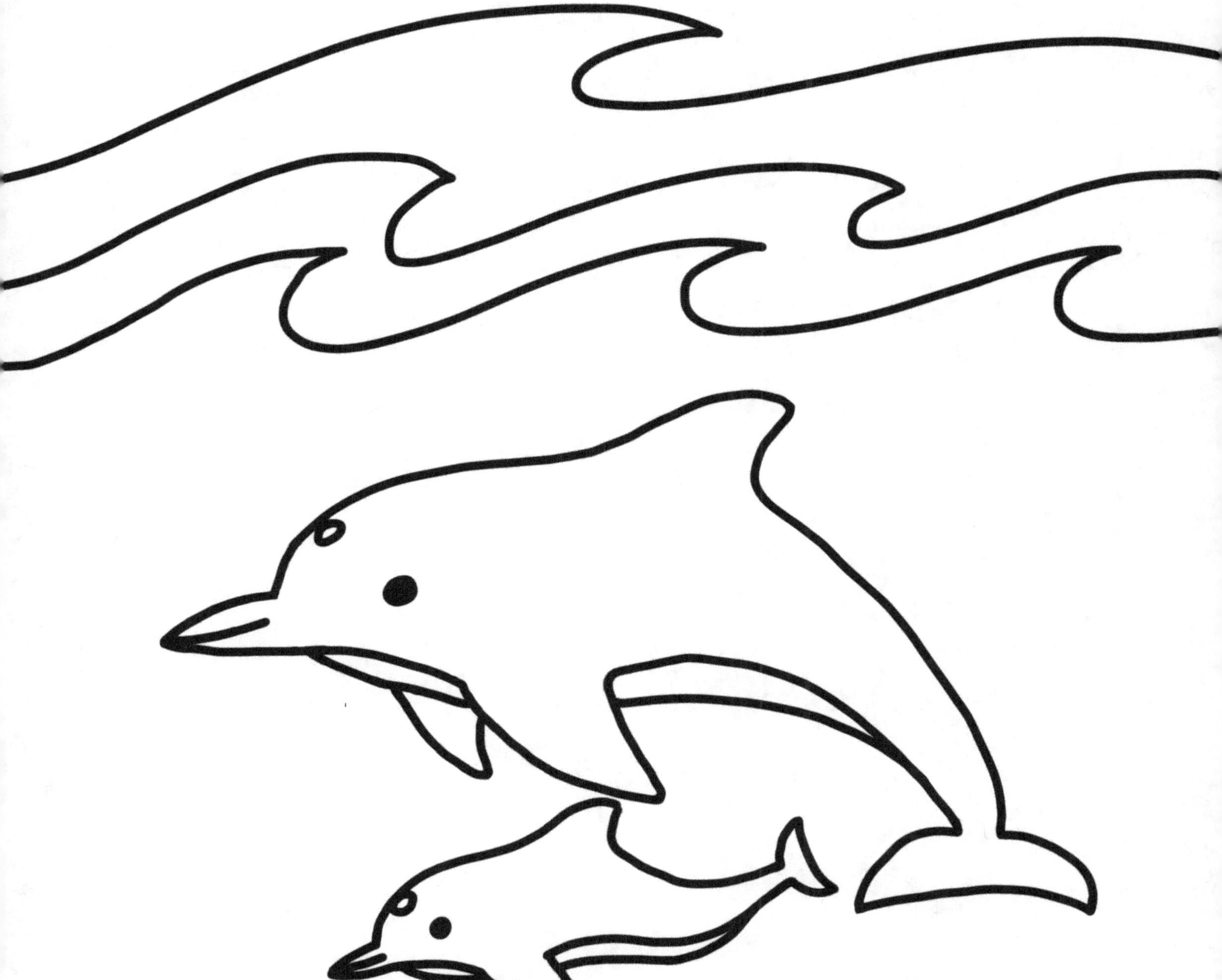

NAI'A

HERMIT CRAB

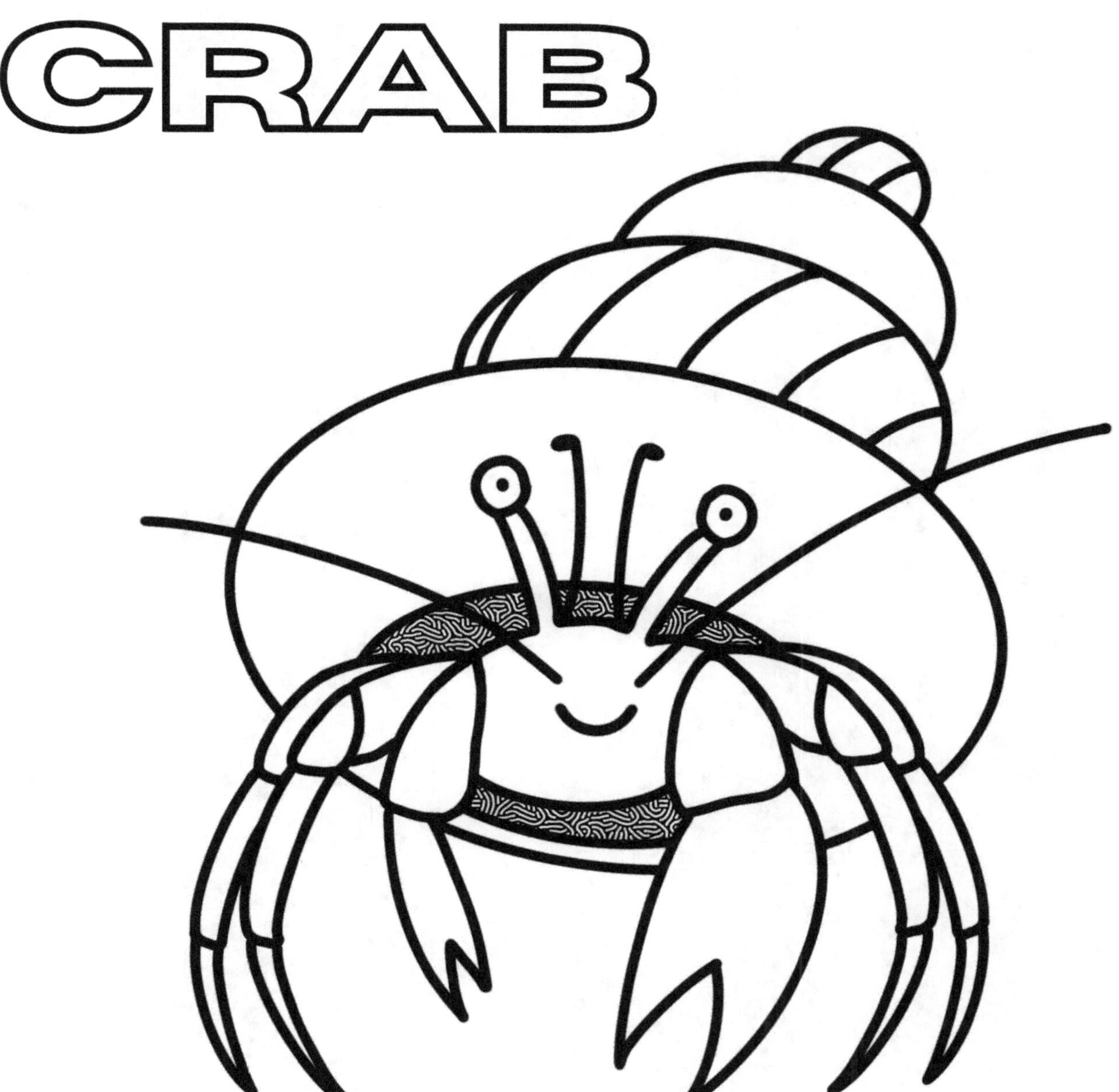

UNAUNA

BOXFISH

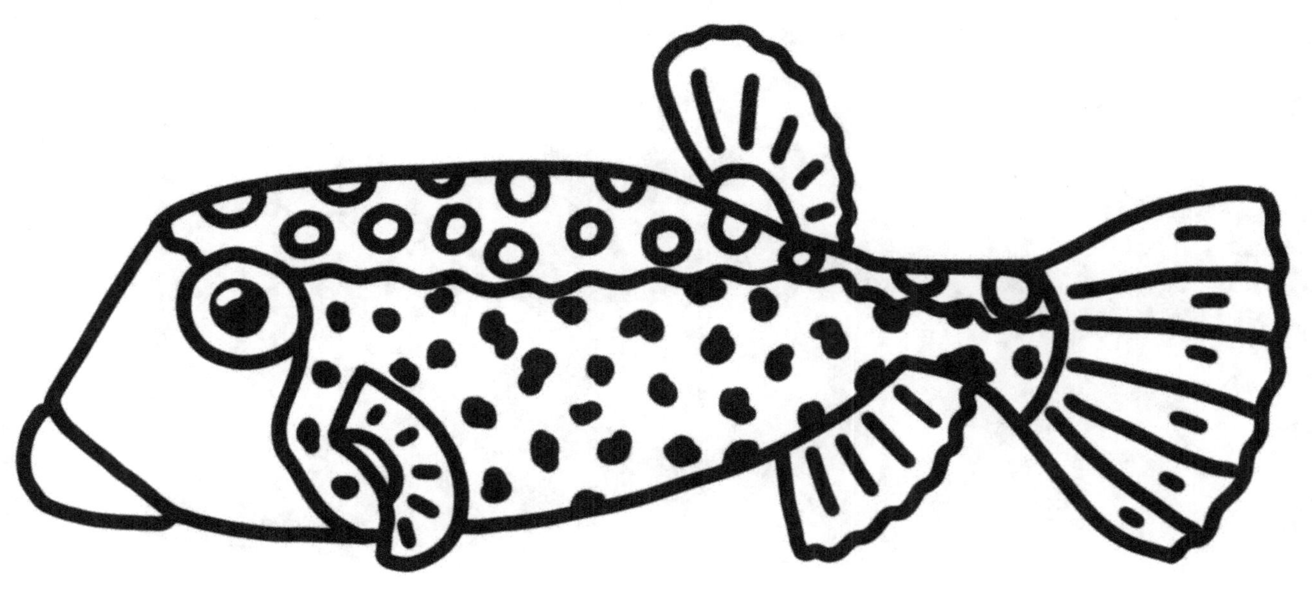

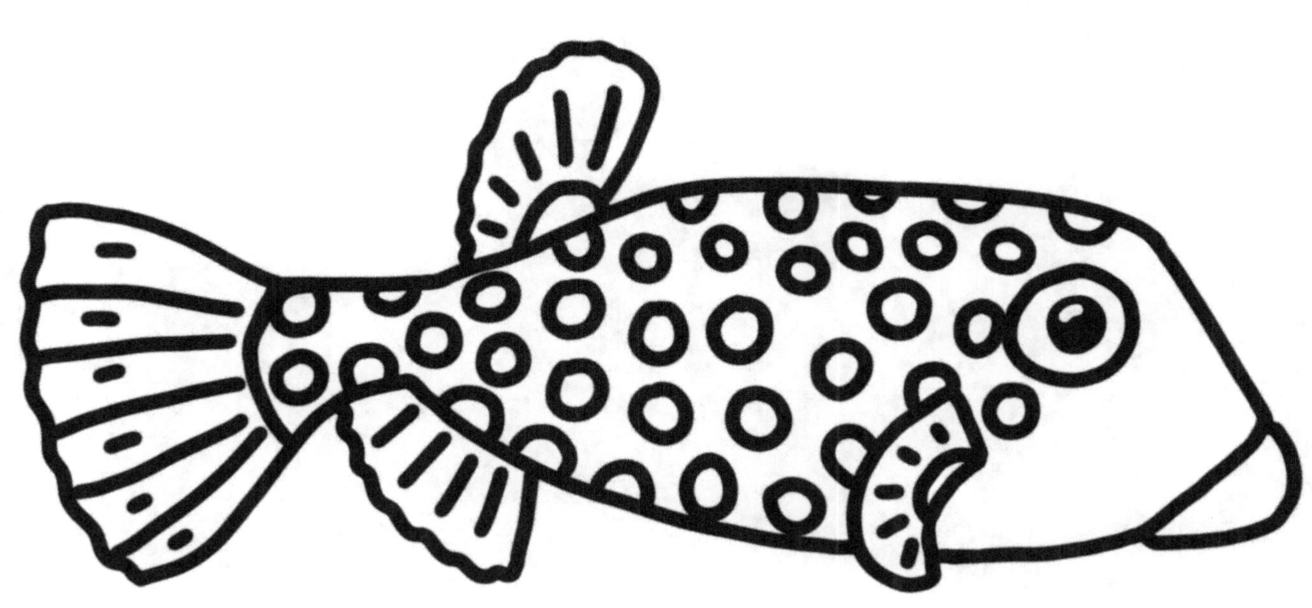

MOA

JELLYFISH

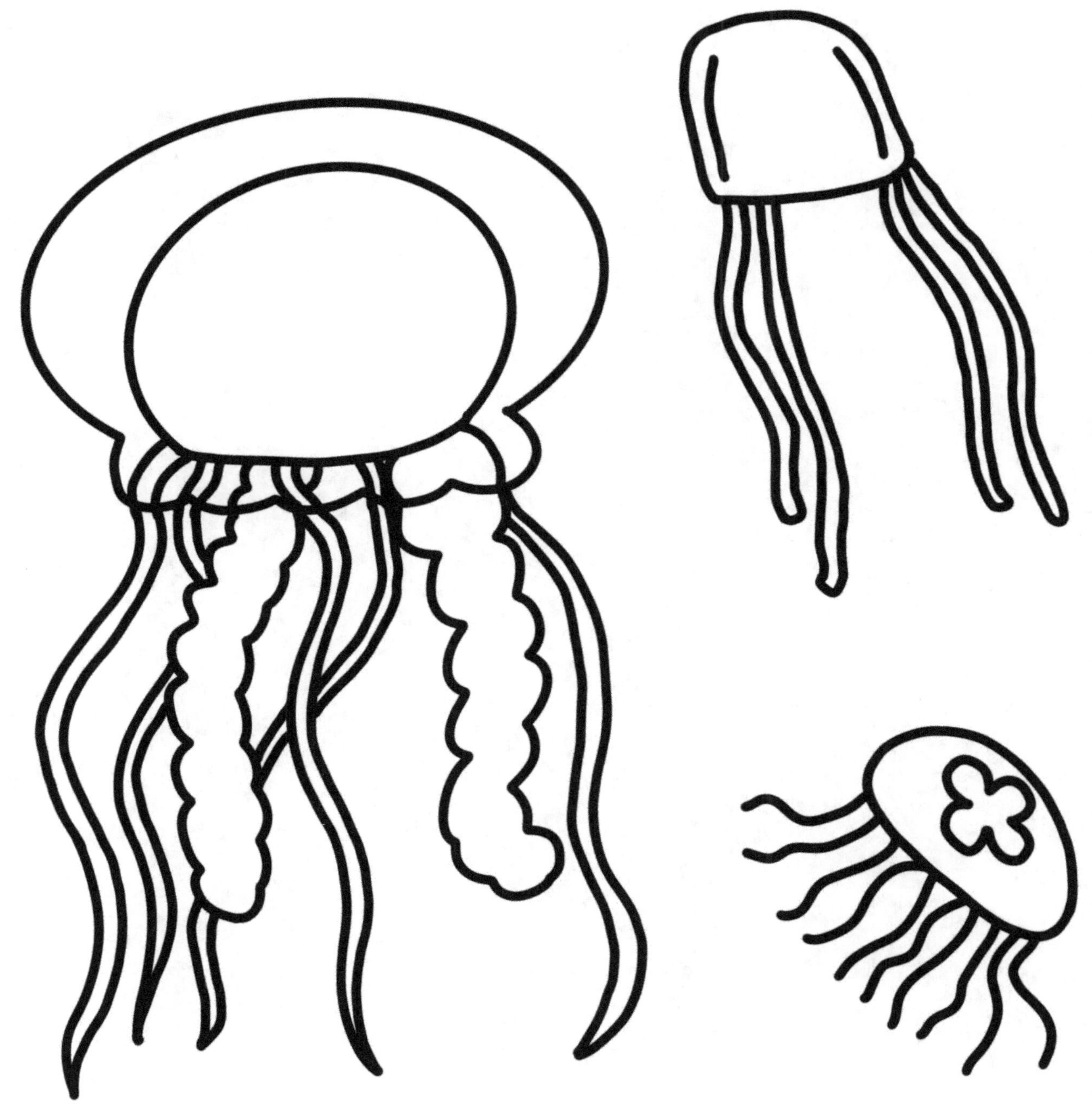

POLOLIA

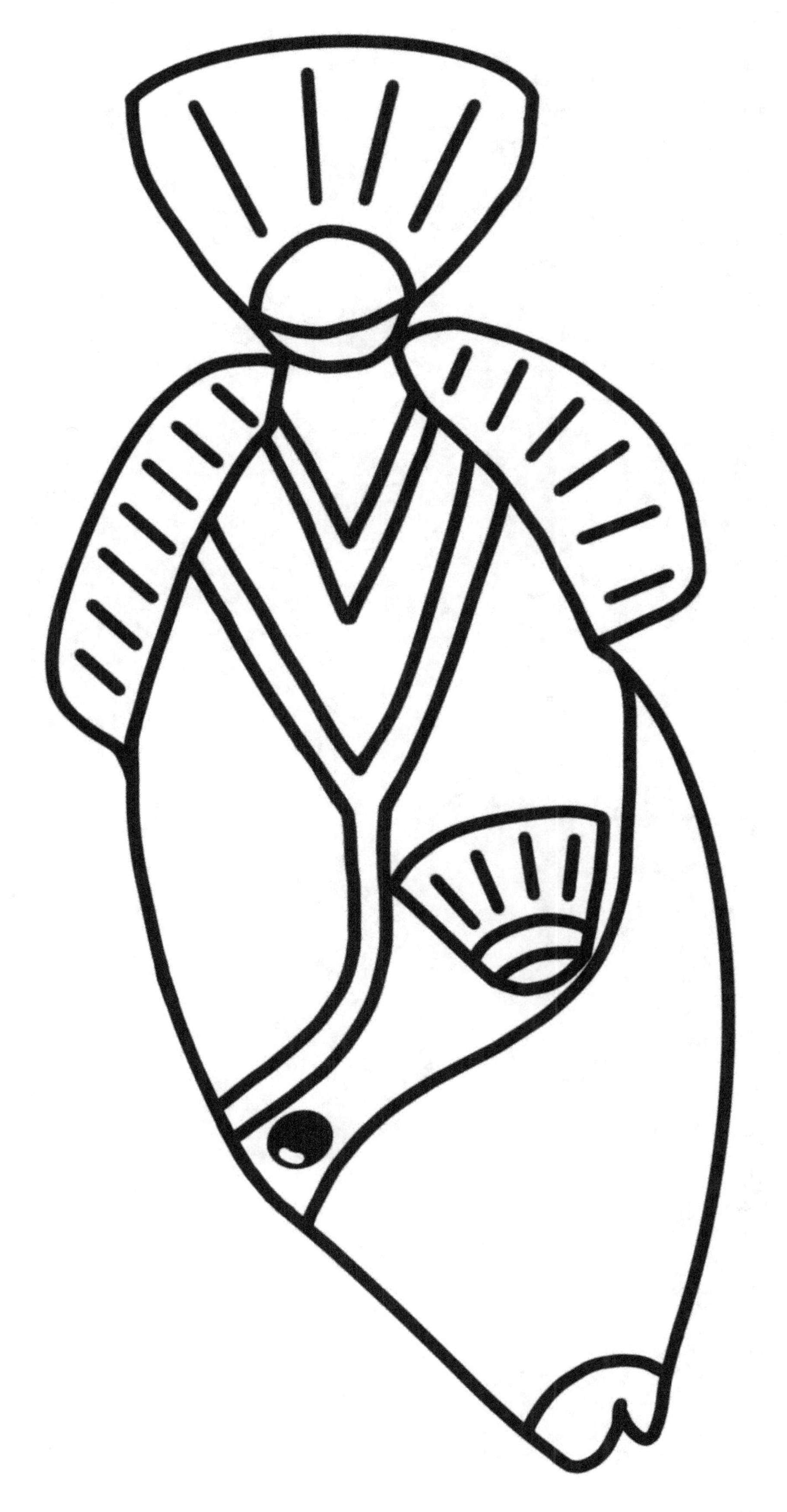
NUKUNUKUʻĀPUAʻA
TRIGGGERFISH
HUMUHUMU

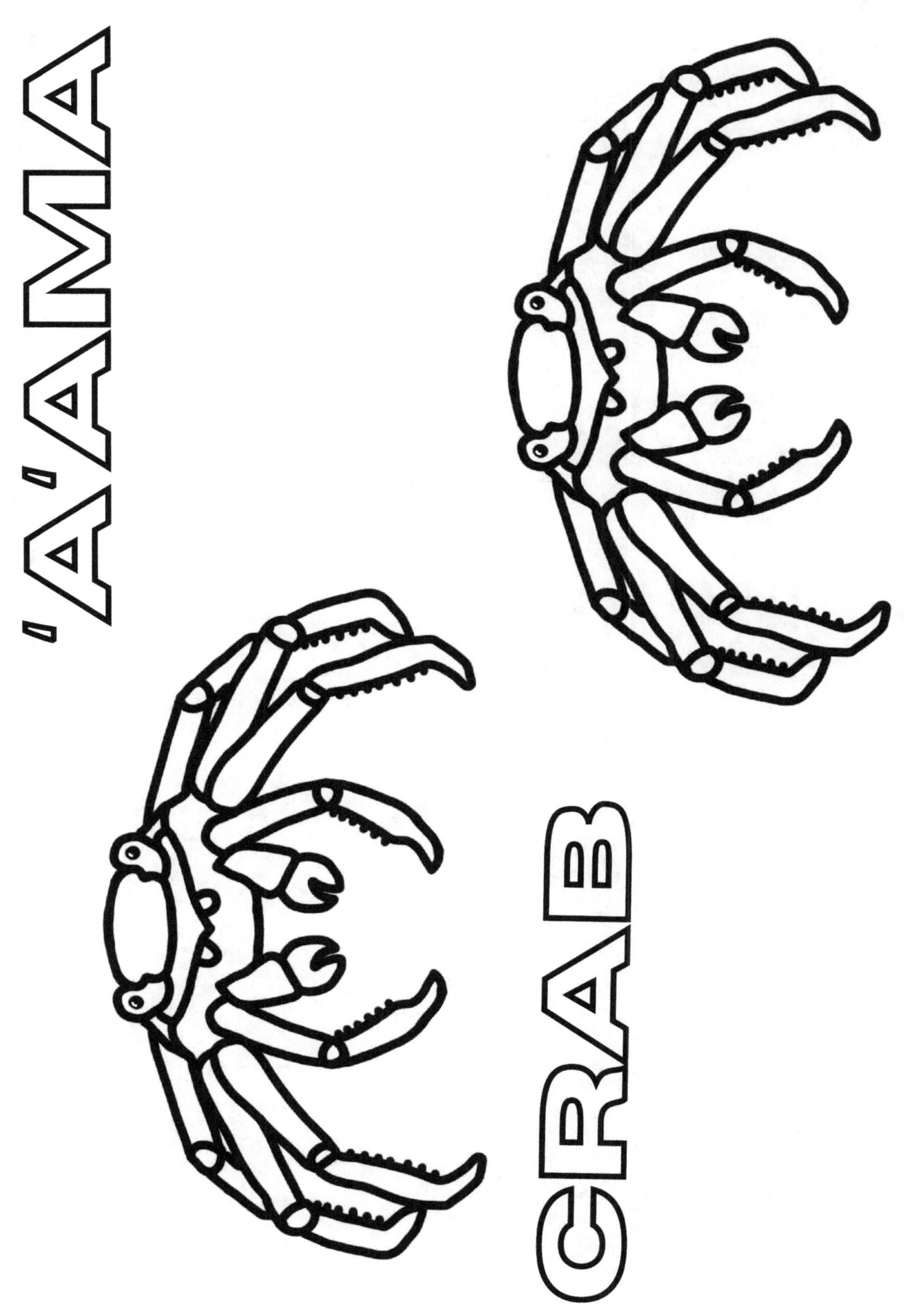

'A'AMA
CRAB

SEAWEED

LIMU

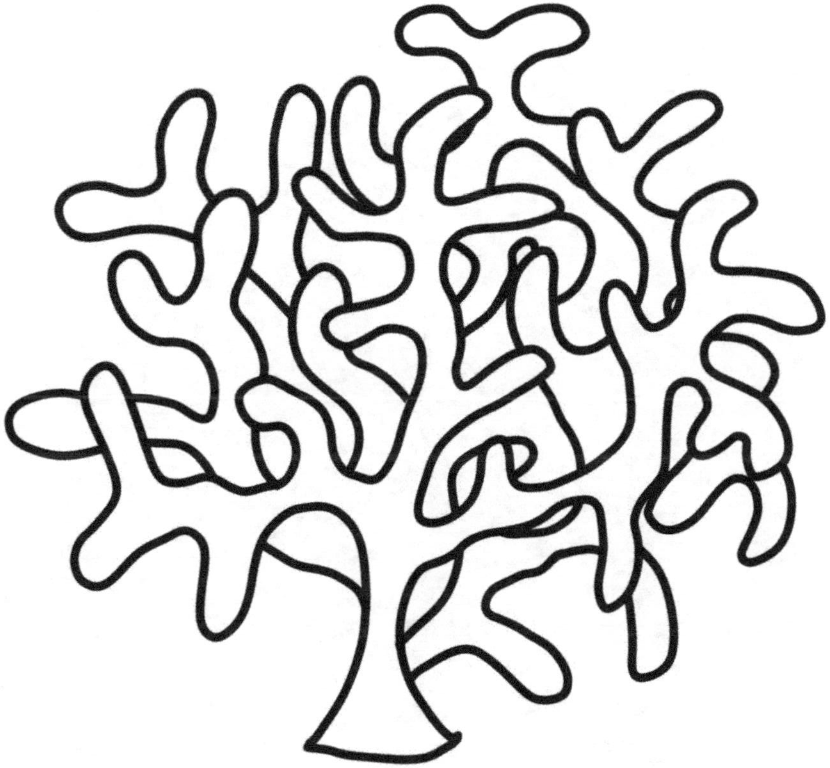

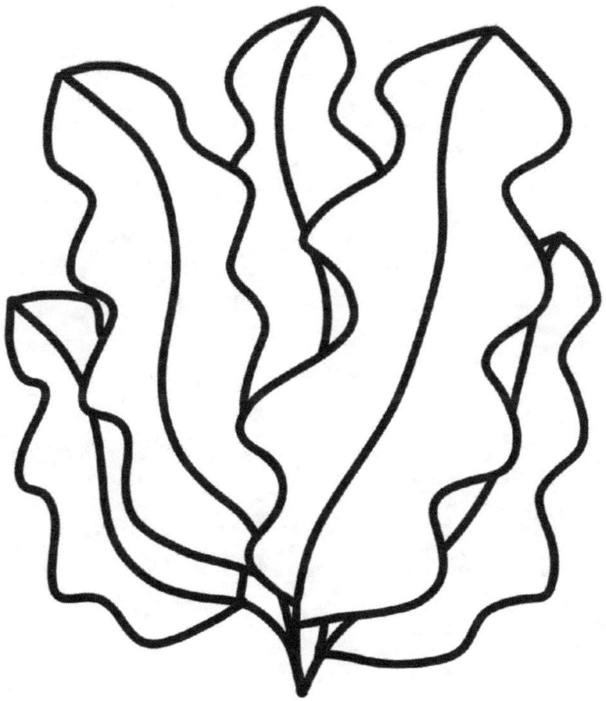

HUMPBACK WHALE

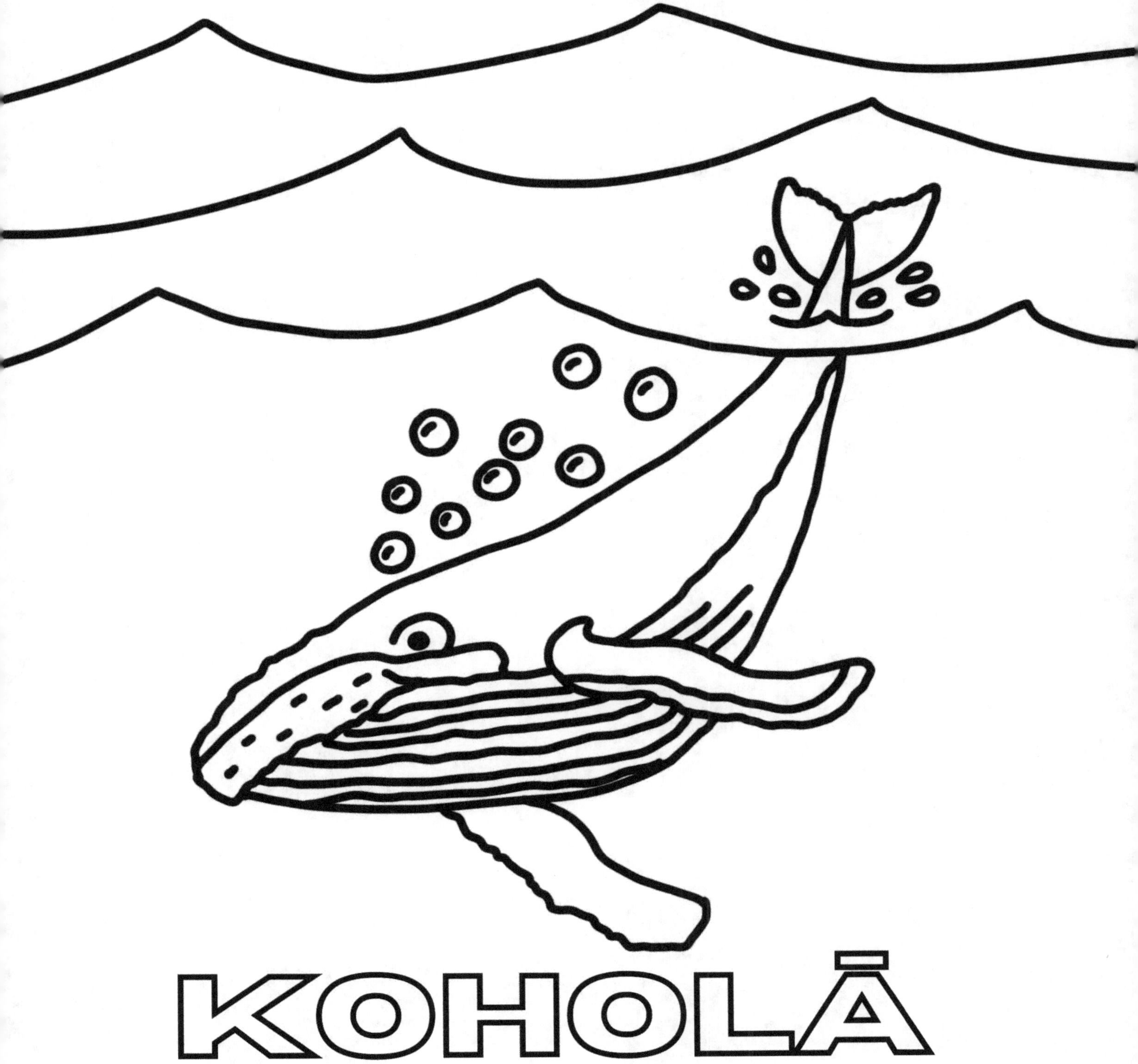

KOHOLĀ

CONVICT TANG

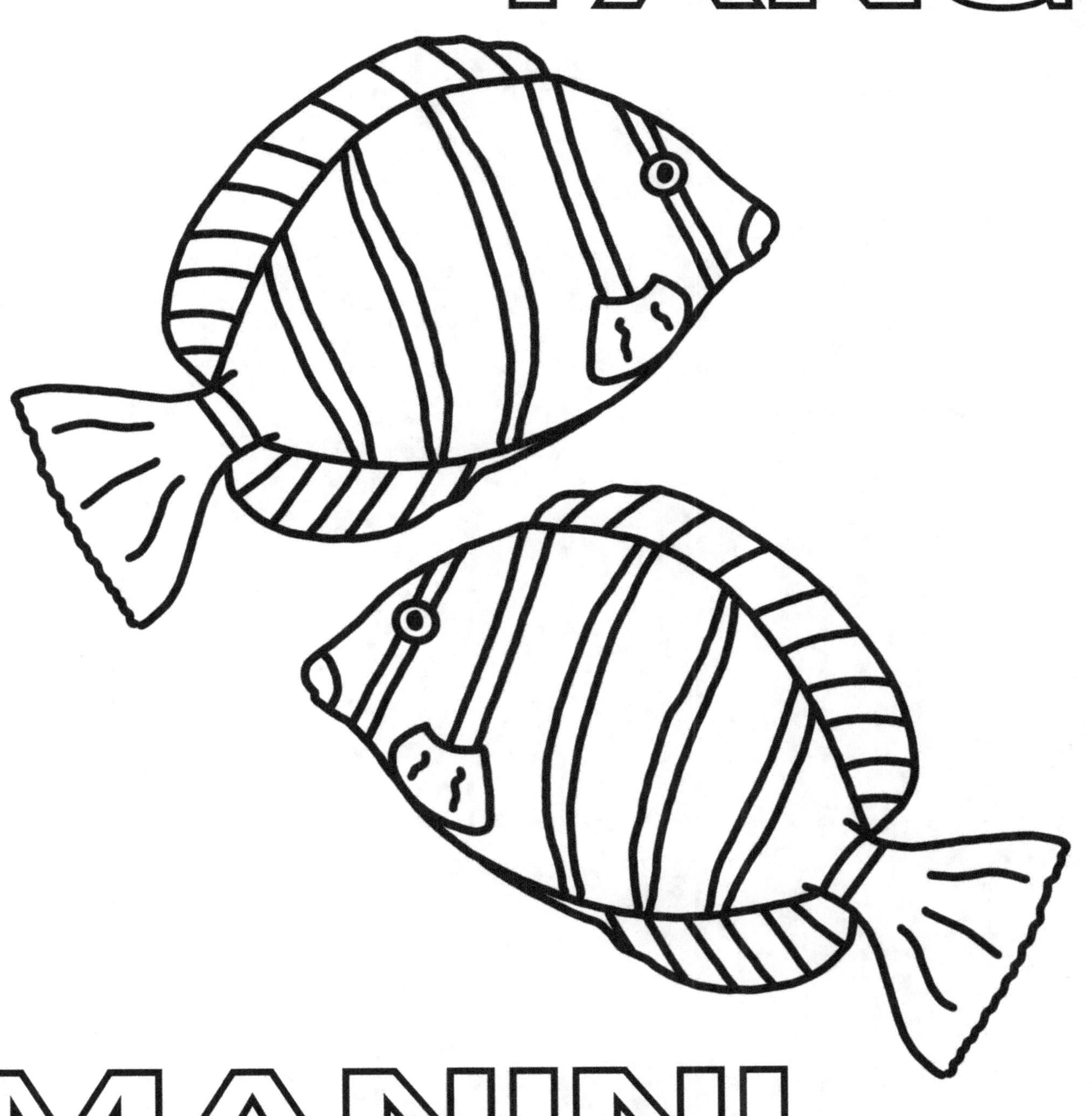

MANINI

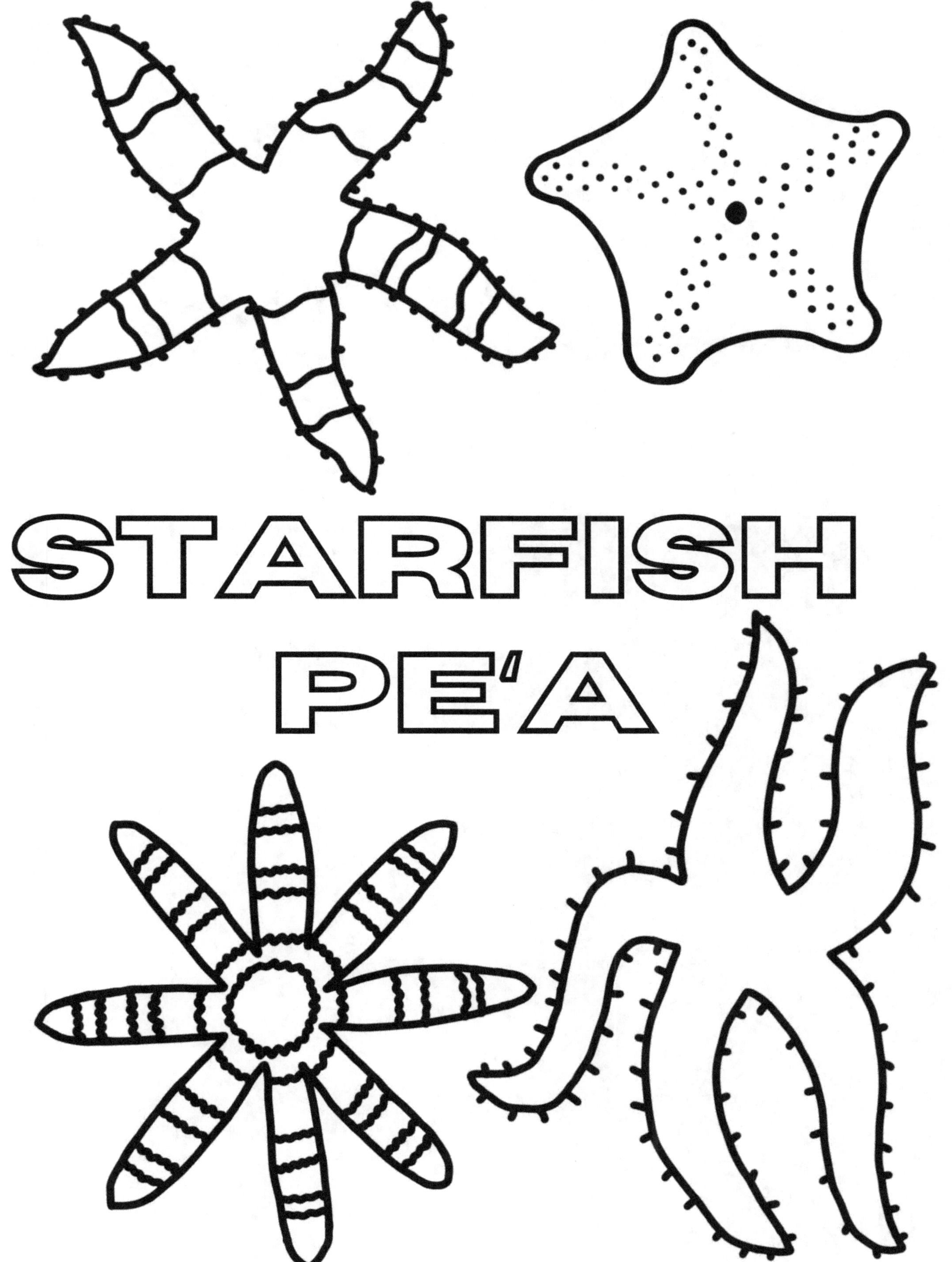

STARFISH
PE'A

YELLOW-FIN TUNA

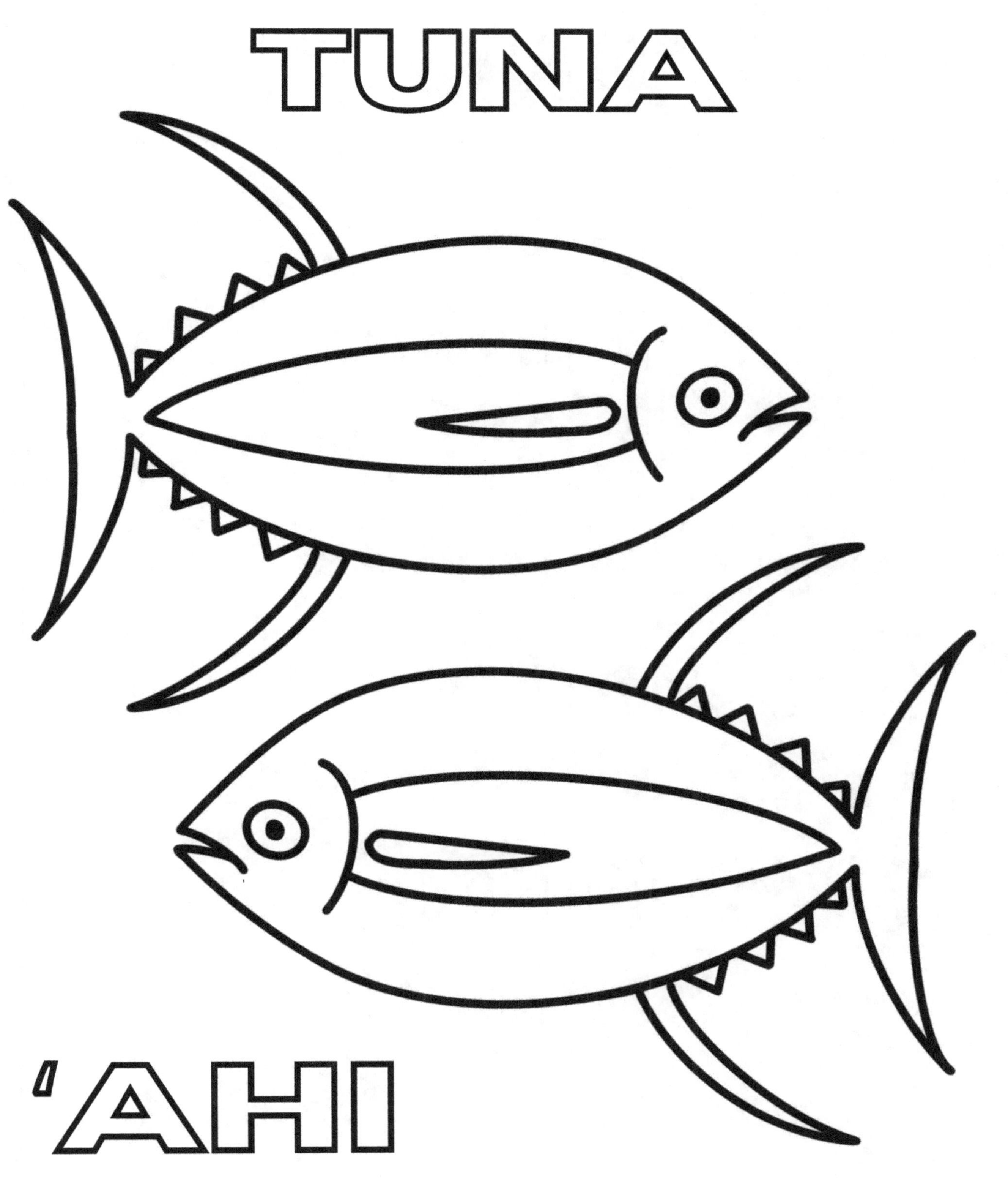

'AHI

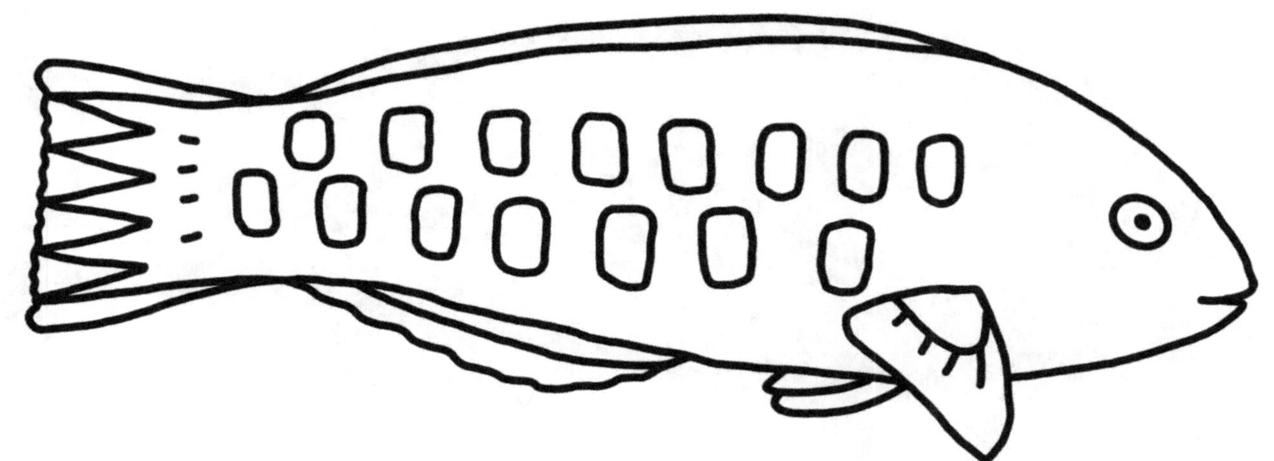

WRASSE

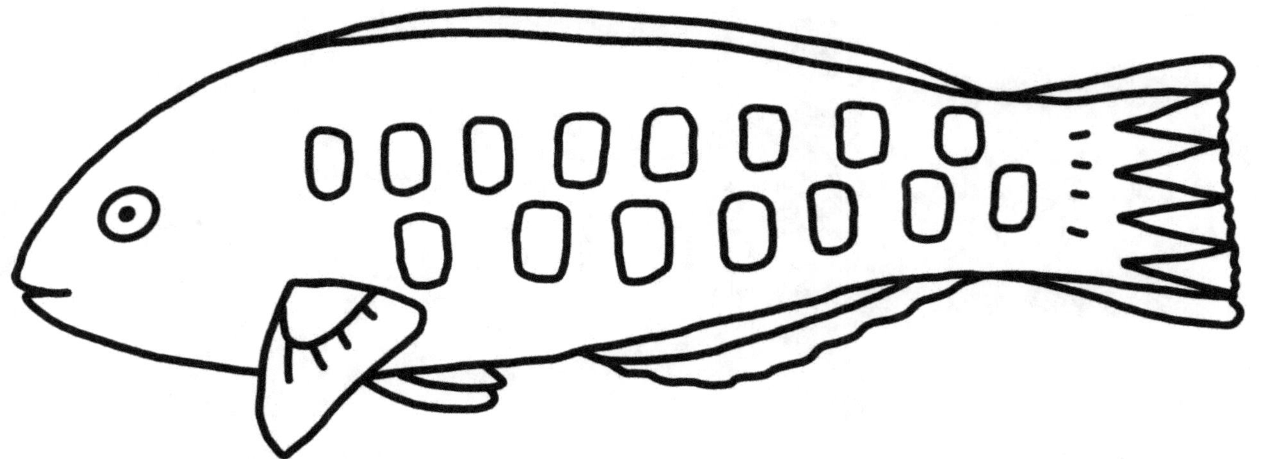

HĪNĀLEA

ʻĪLIO HOLO I KA UAUA

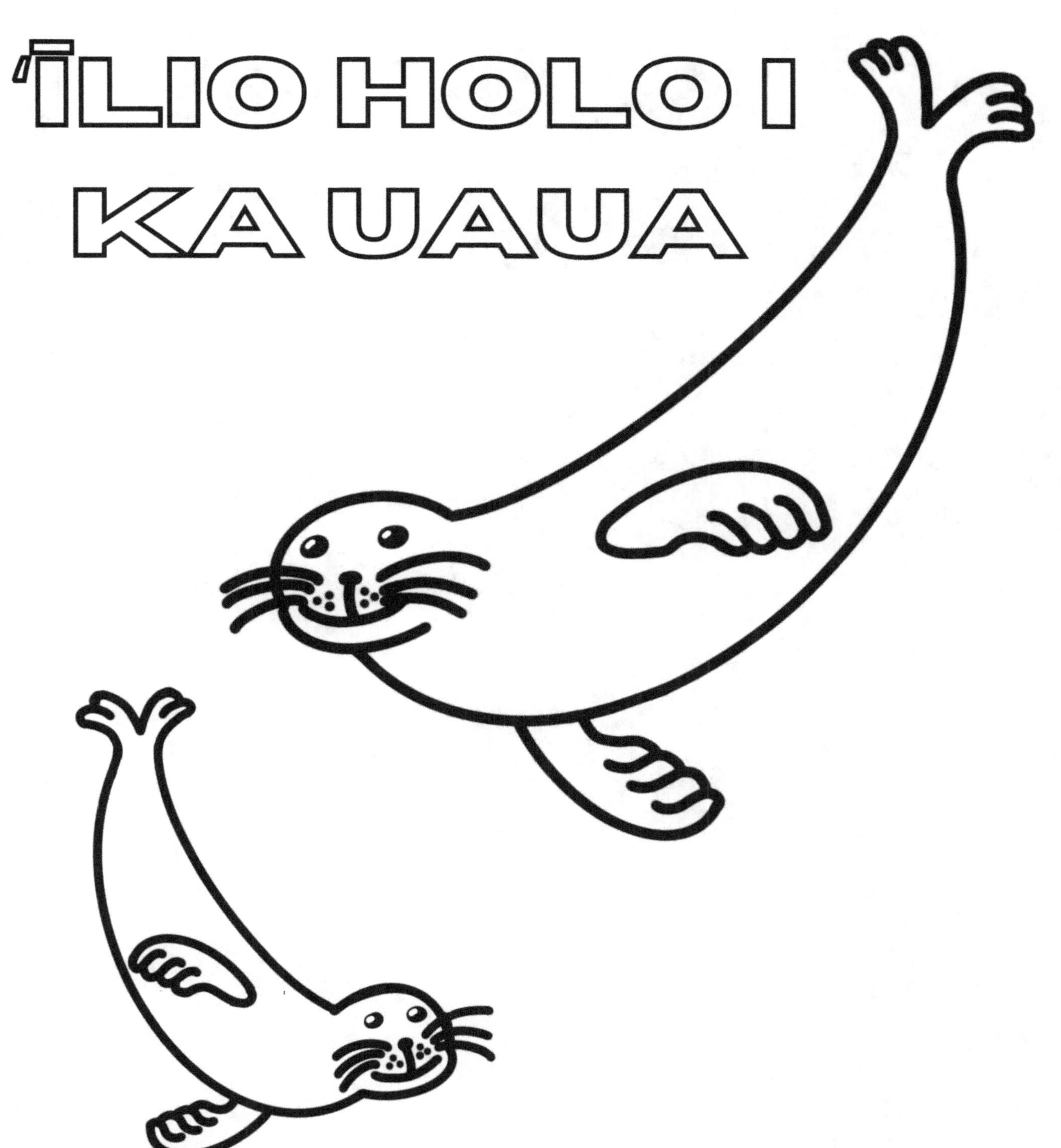

HAWAIIAN MONK SEAL

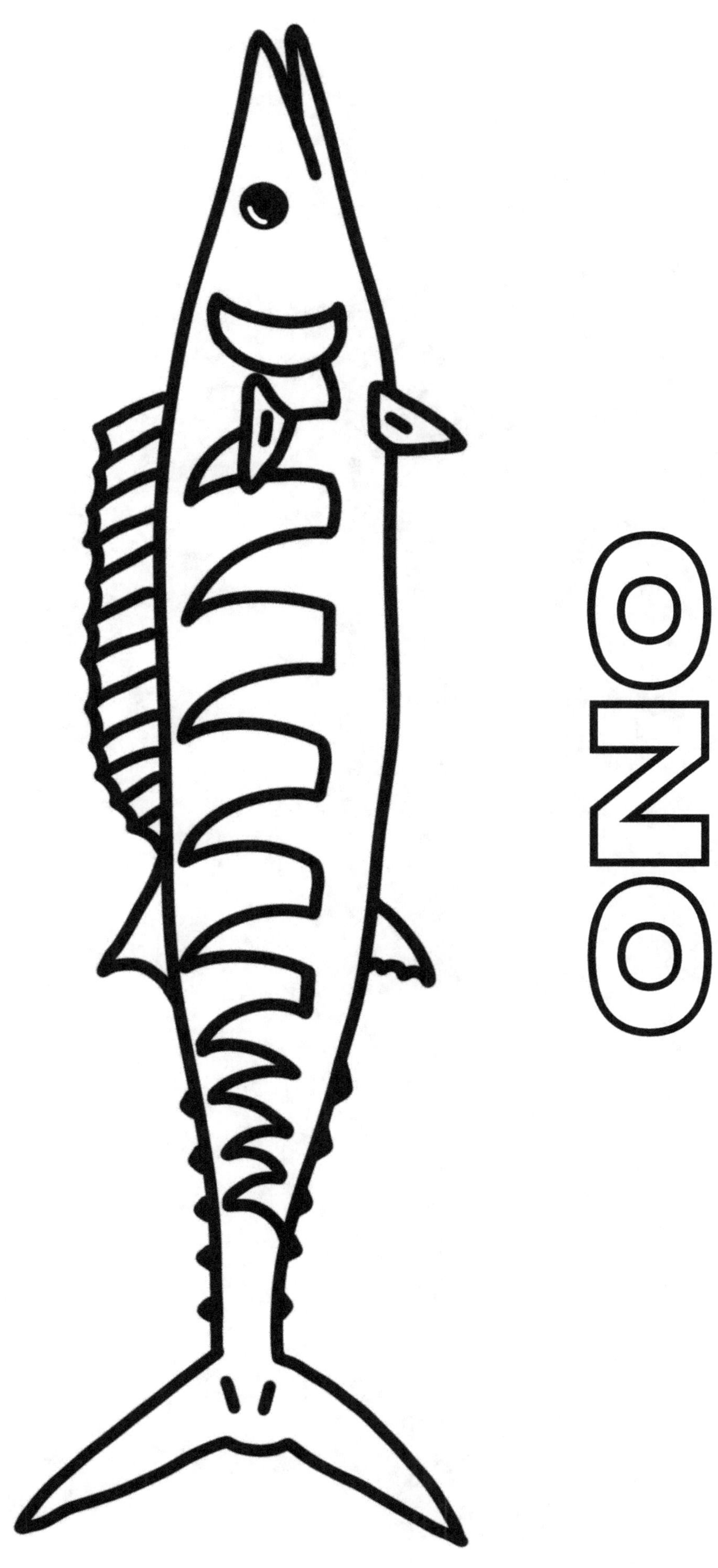

WAHOO
ONO

'ŌKALA

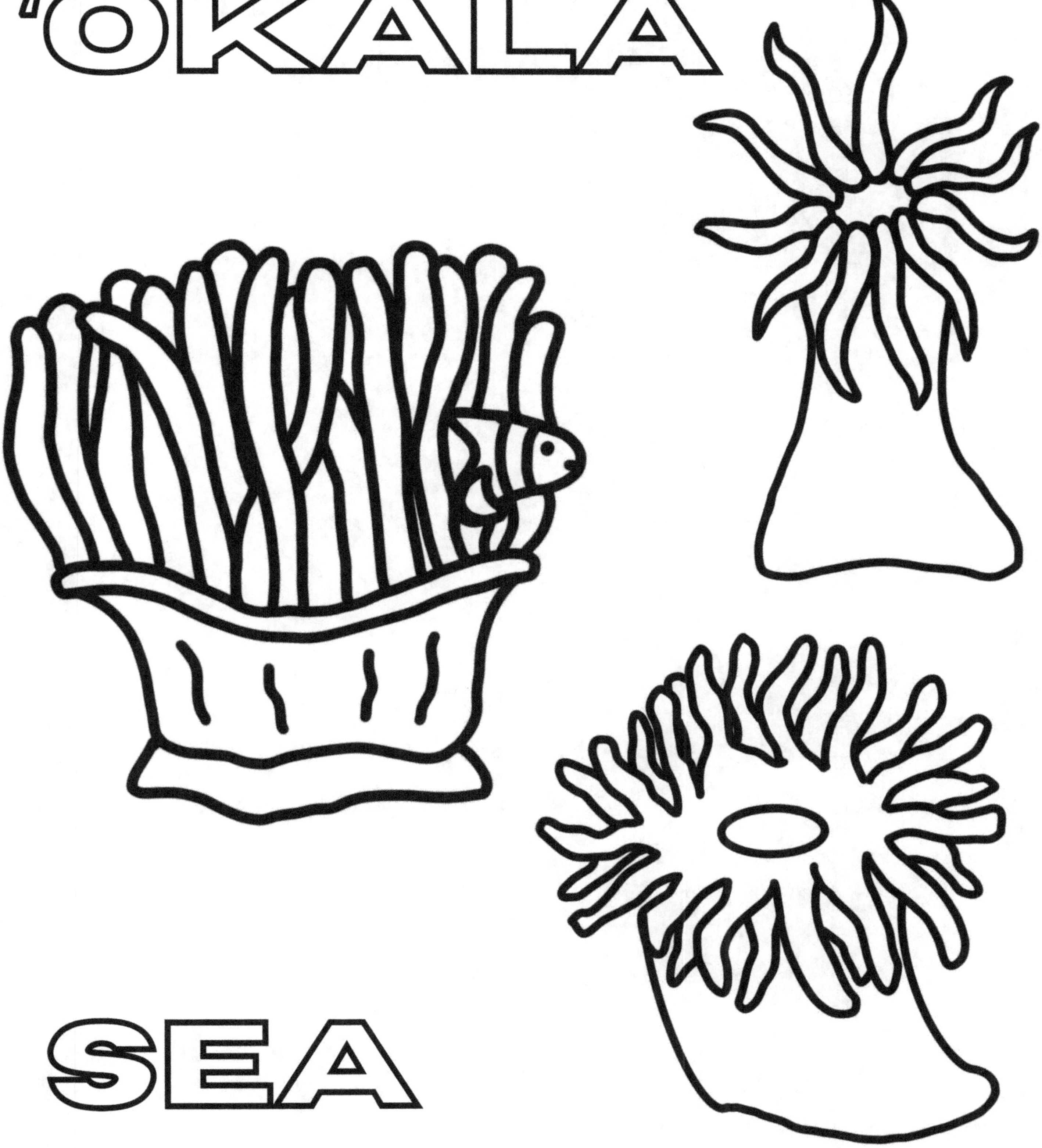

SEA
ANEMONE

MARLIN

A'U

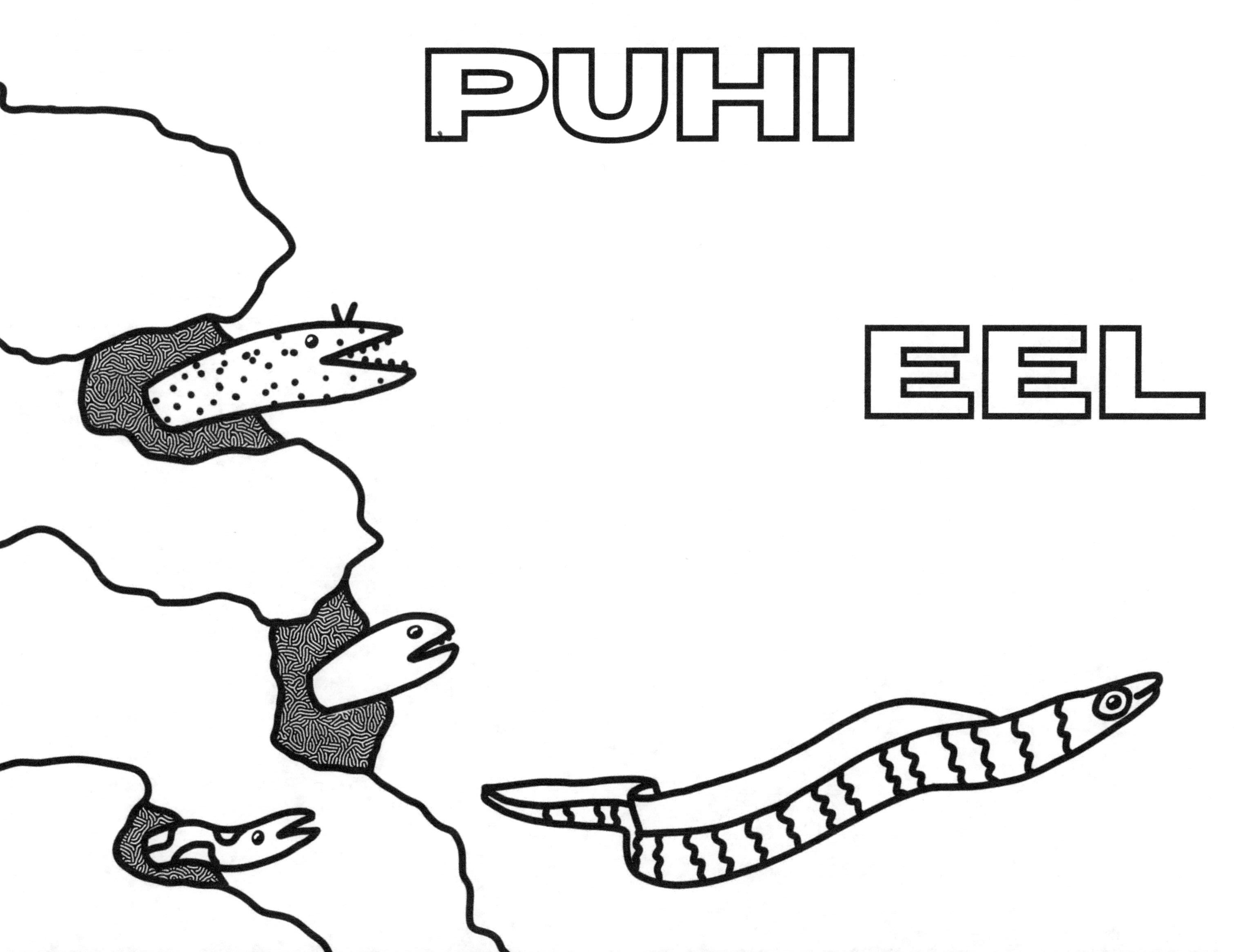

PUHI
EEL

HONU

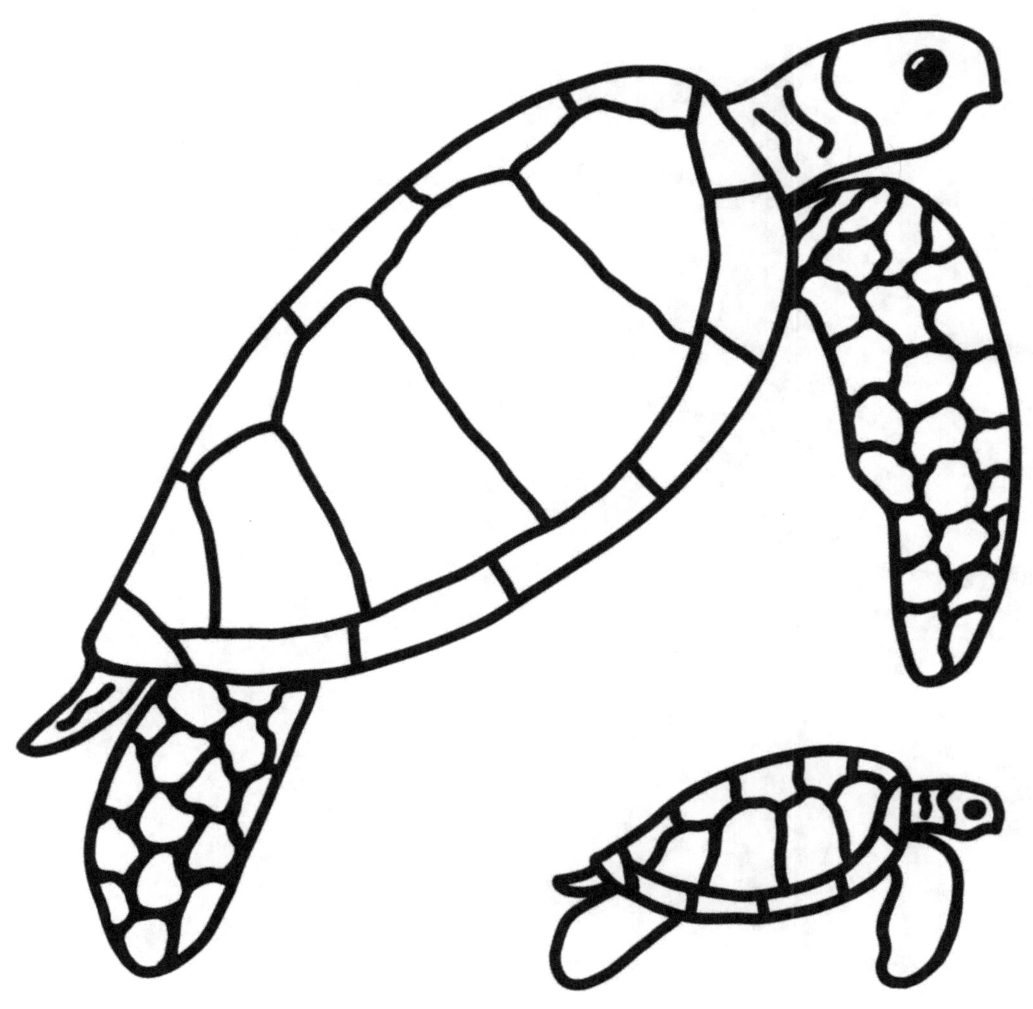

GREEN SEA
TURTLE

SLATE PENCIL URCHIN

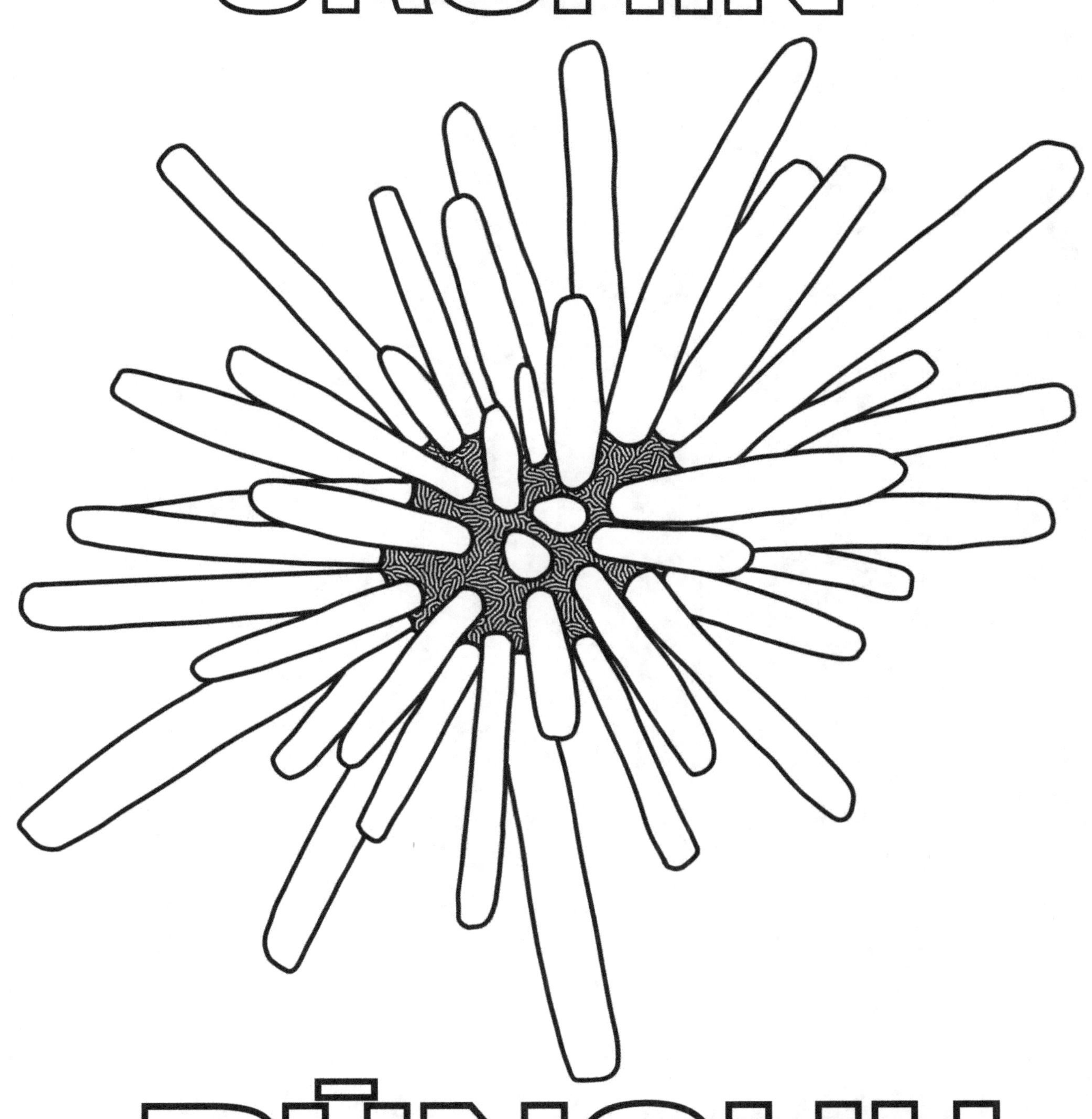

PŪNOHU

OCTOPUS

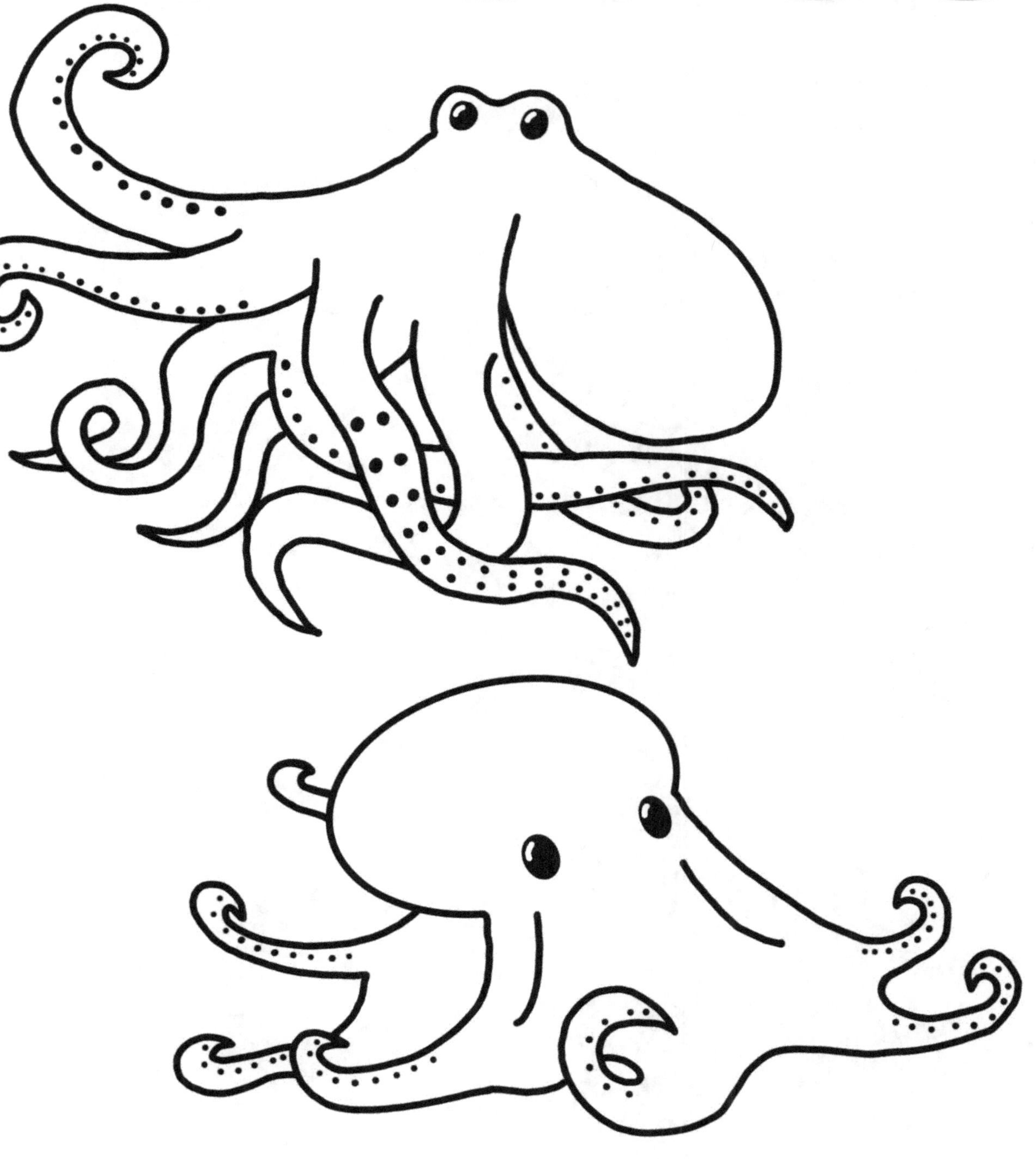

HE'E

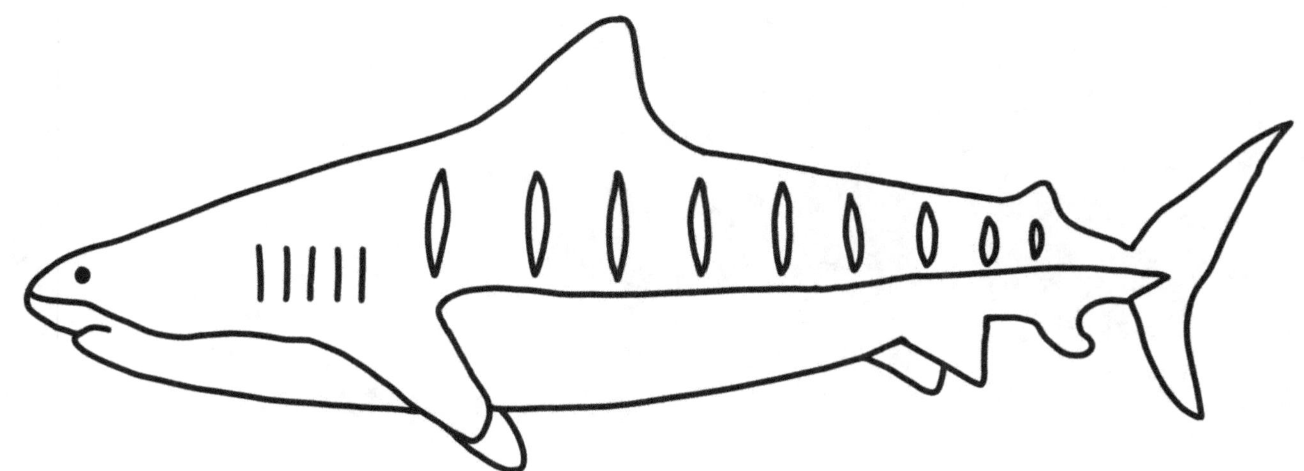

MANŌ

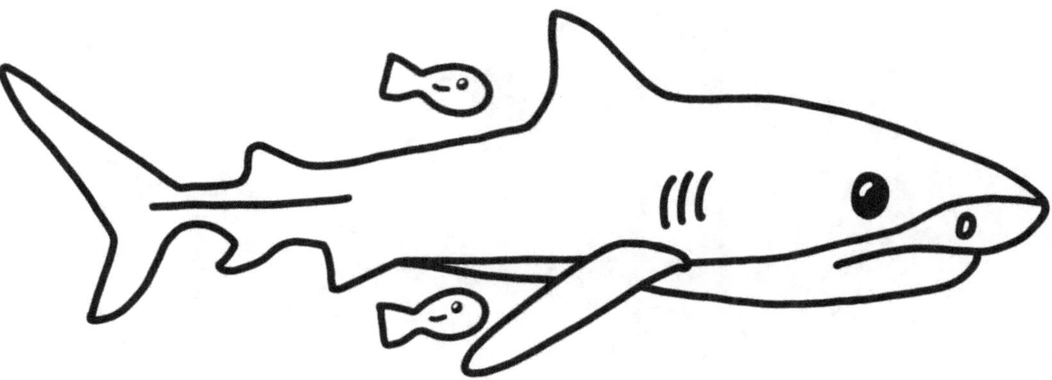

SHARK

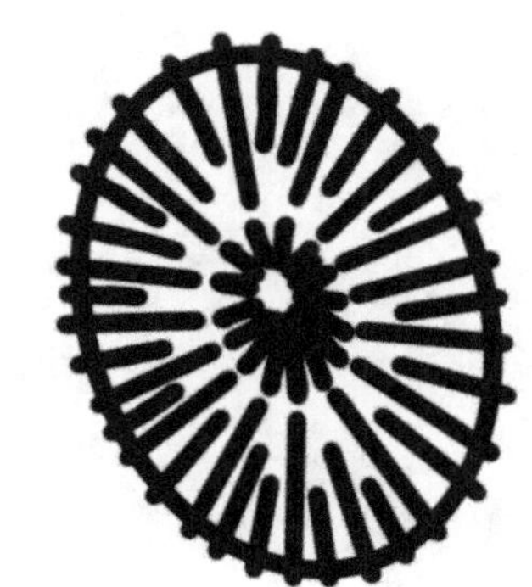
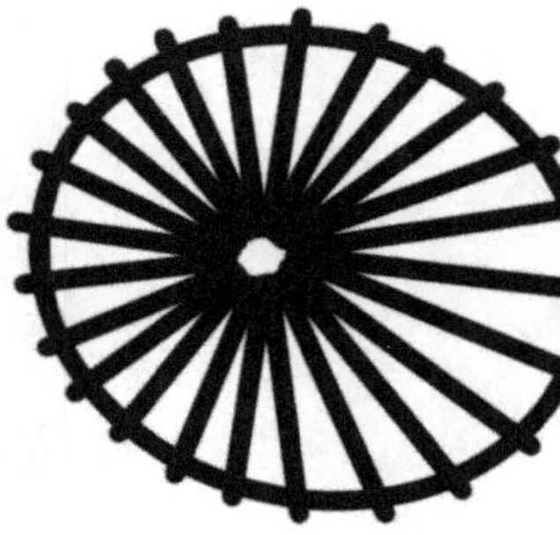
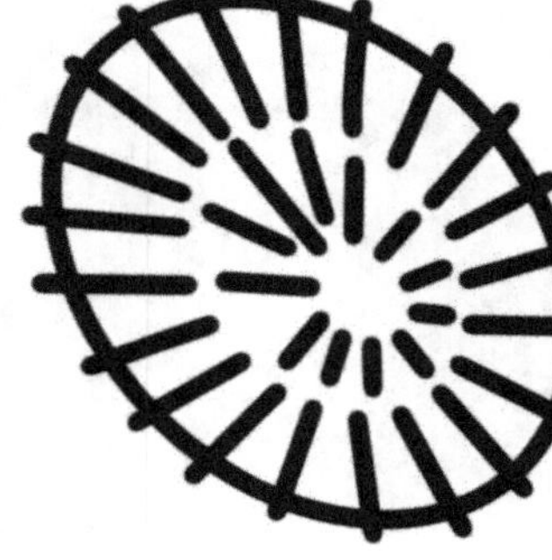

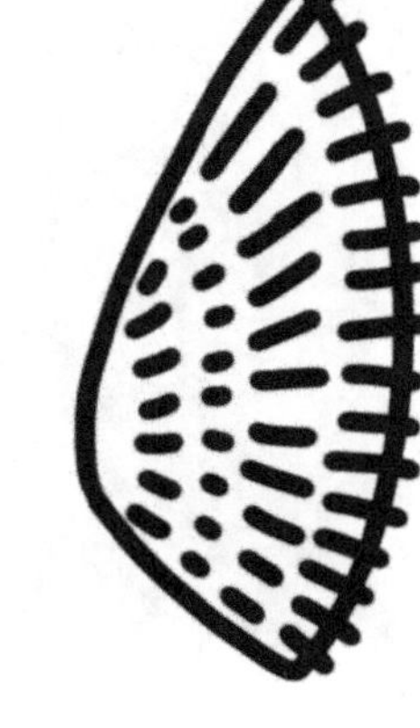
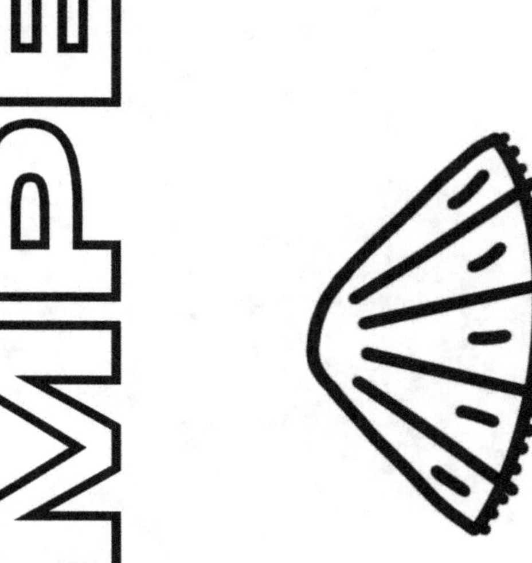
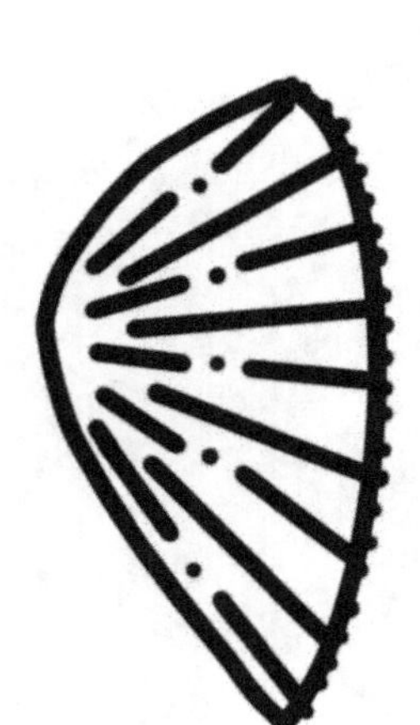
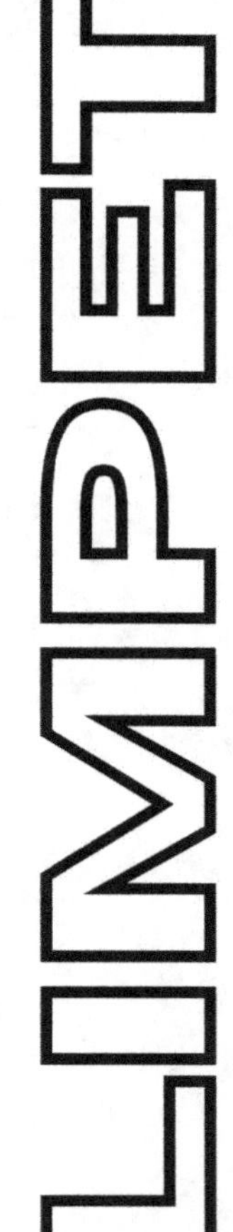

ʻOPIHI

LIMPET

CORAL

KO'A

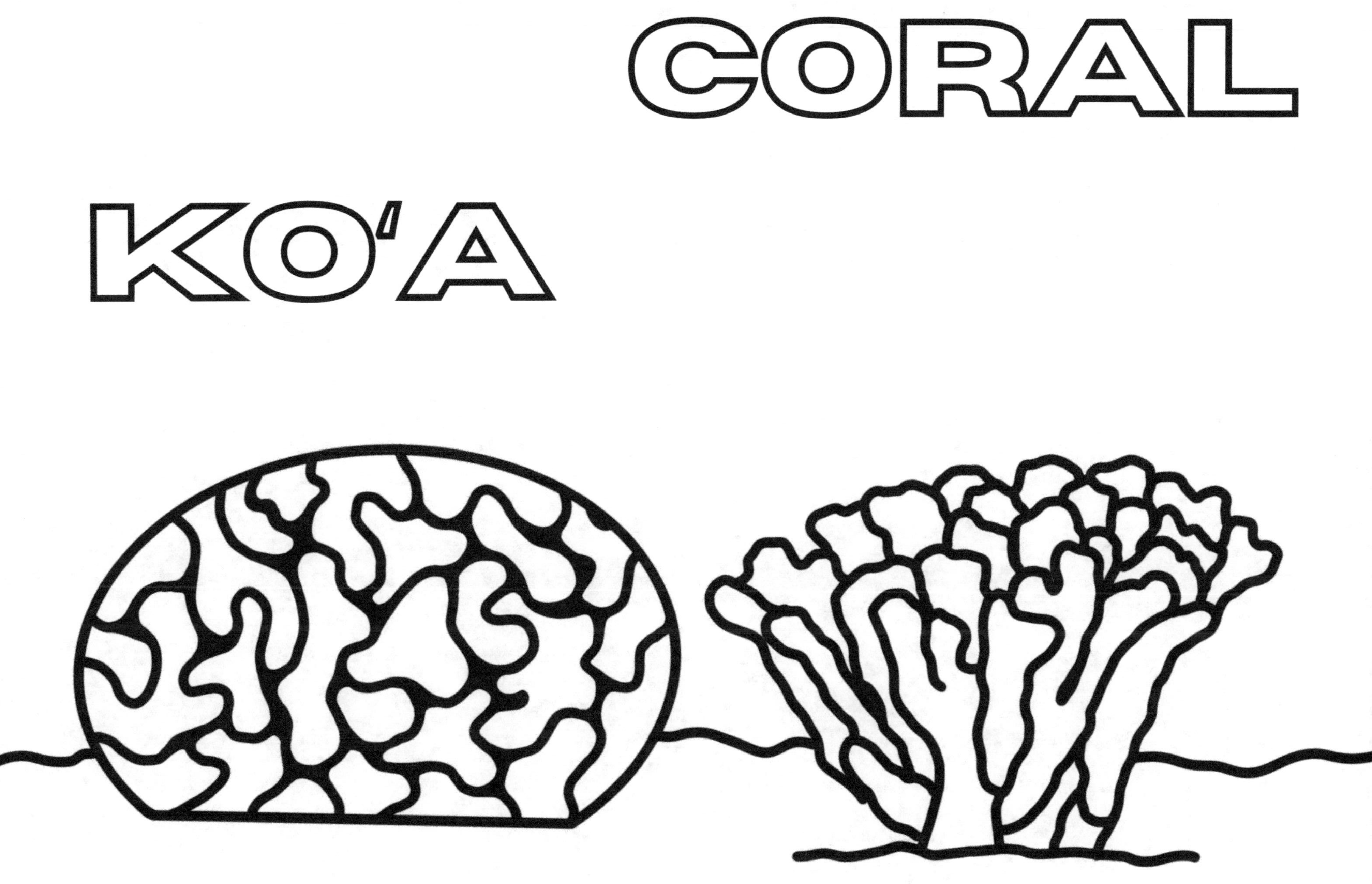

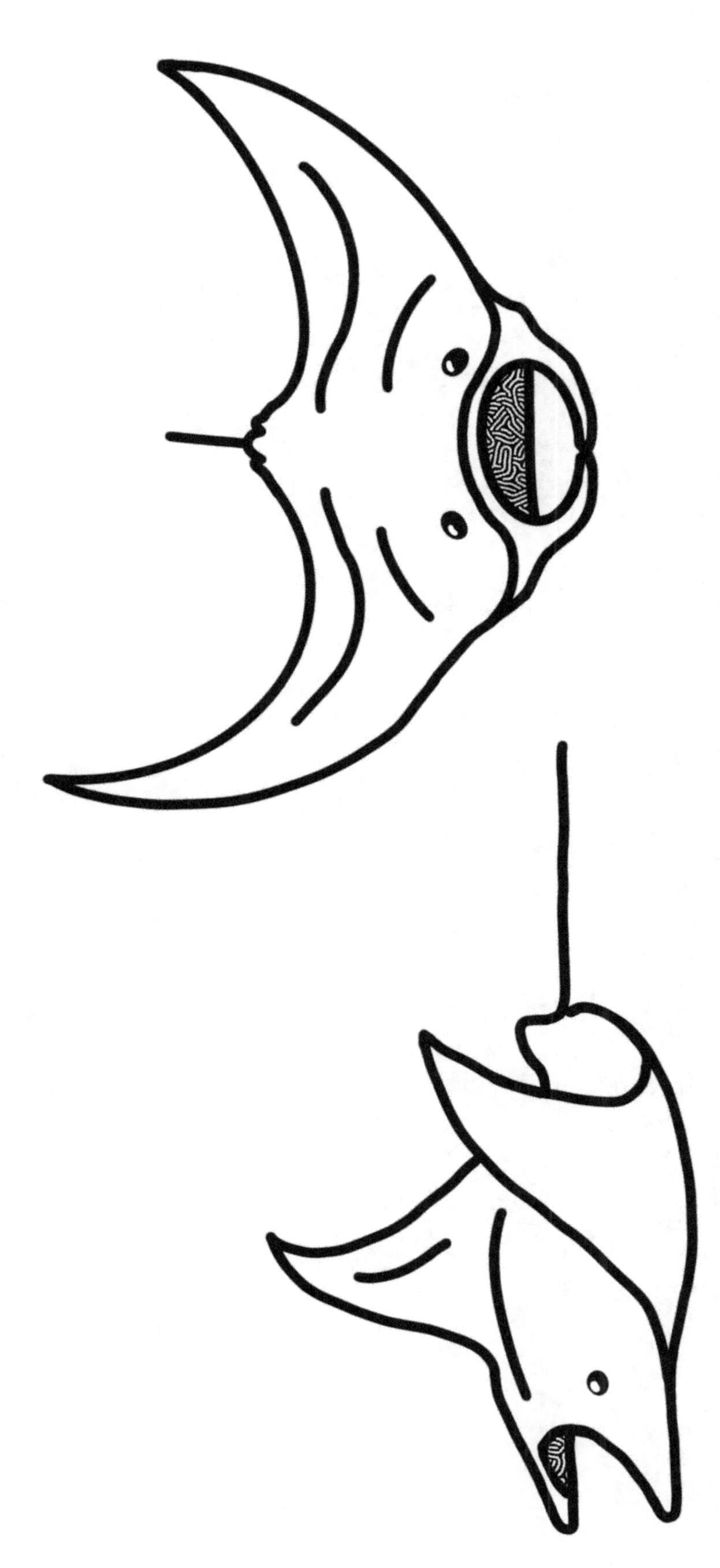

HĀHĀLUA
MANTA RAY

MOORISH IDOL

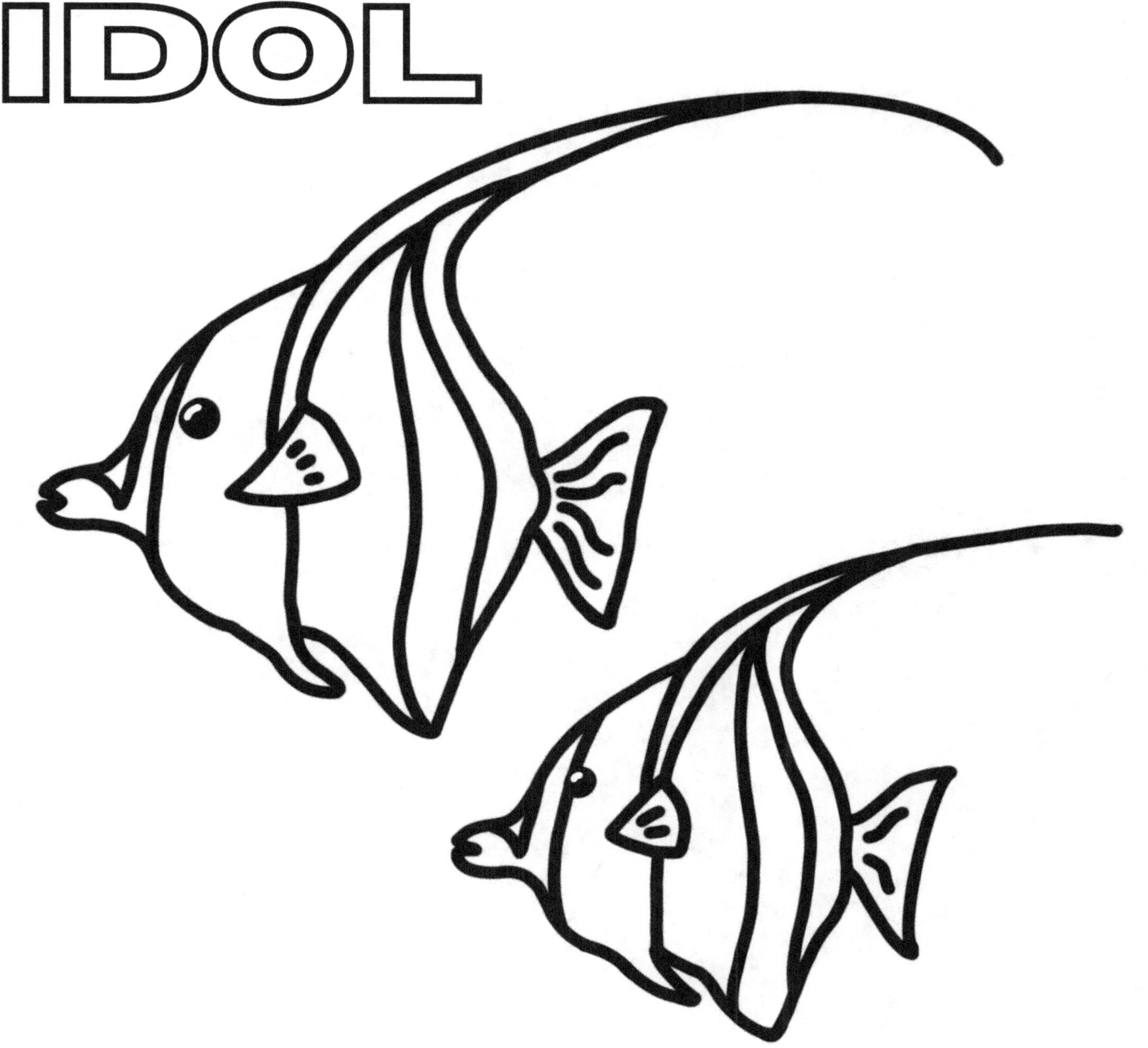

KIHIKIHI

'ŌPAKAPAKA

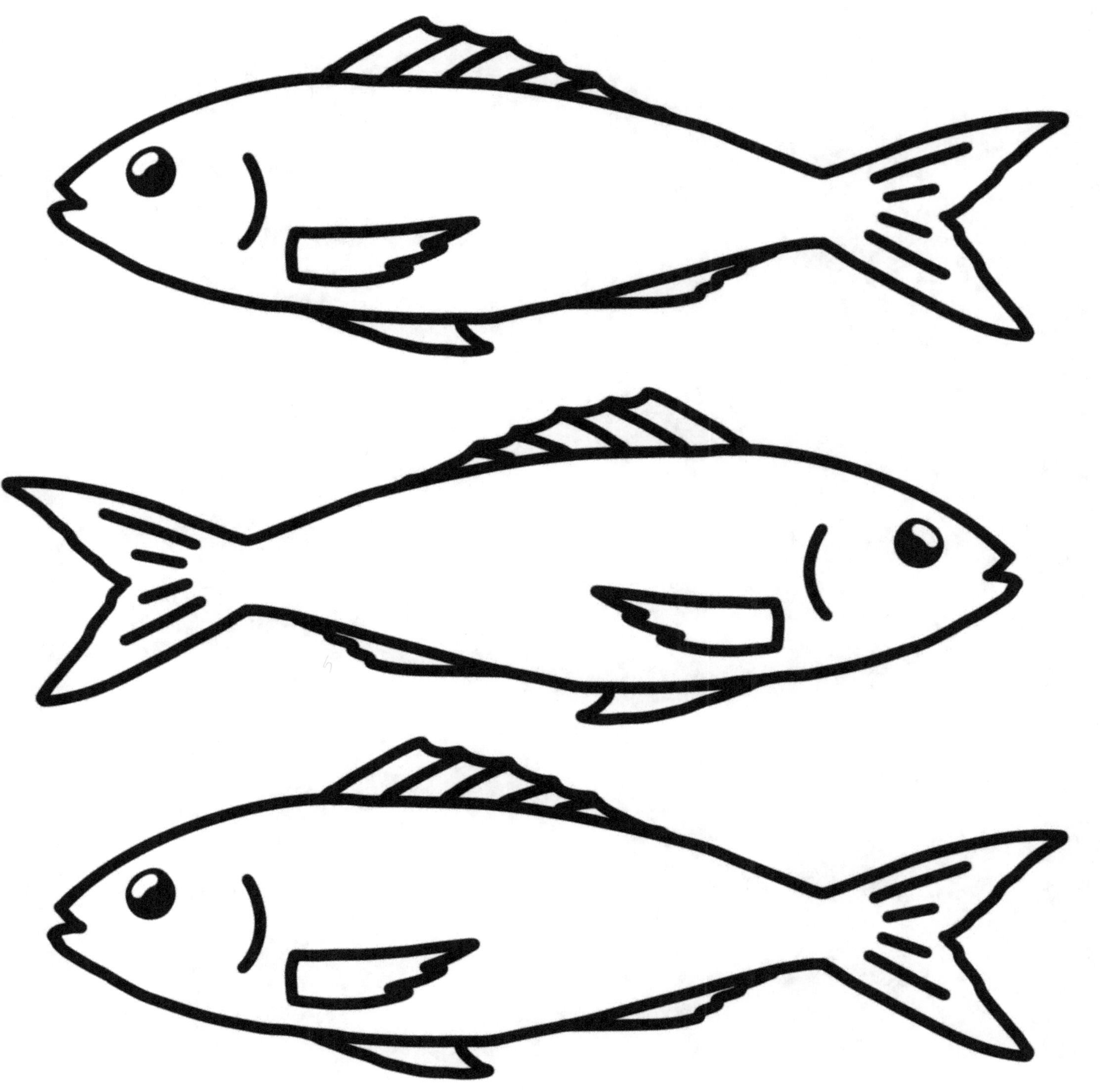

SNAPPER

LAUHAU

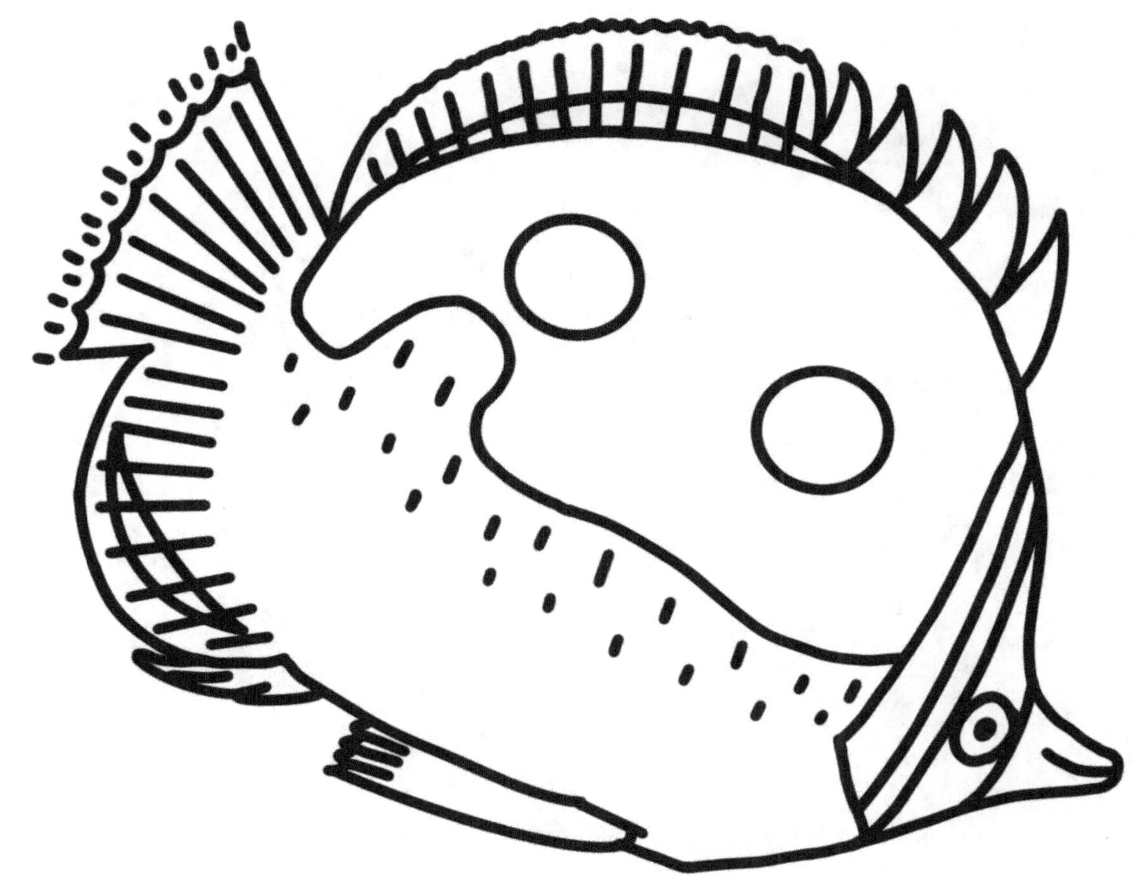

FOURSPOT
BUTTERFLY
FISH

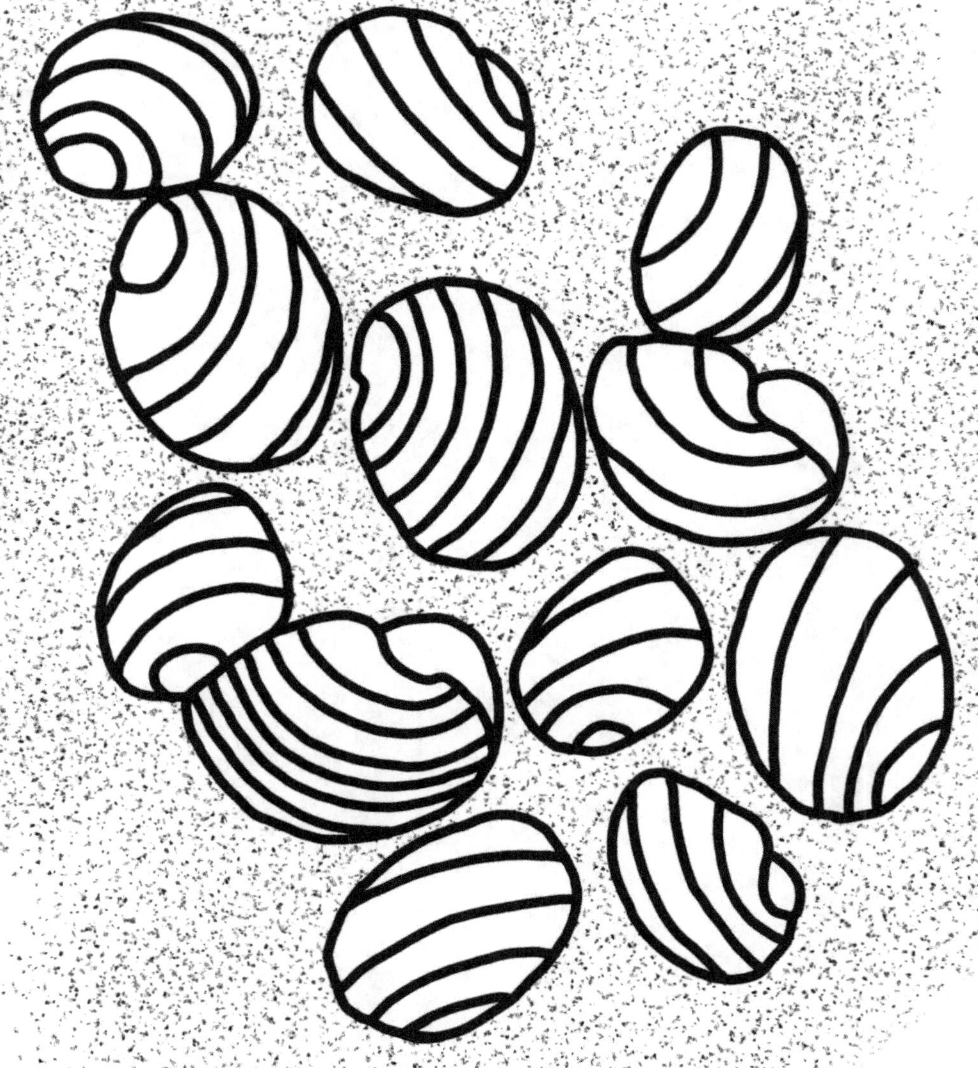

PIPIPI

MOLLUSKS

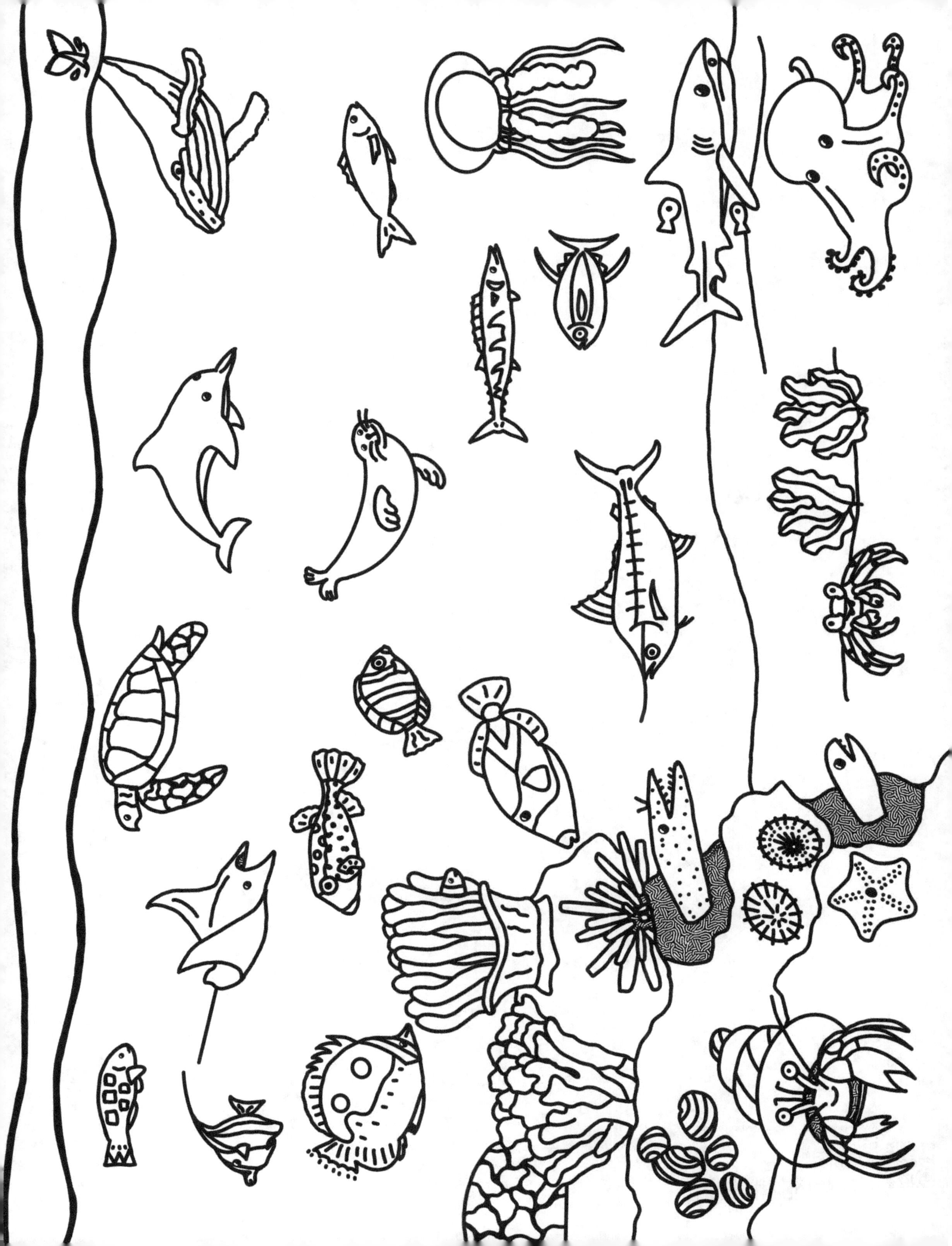